TINY
GOD
SYNDROME

JAKE WALKER

innovo
PUBLISHING

Published by Innovo Publishing, LLC
www.innovopublishing.com
1-888-546-2111

Providing Full-Service Publishing Services for Christian Authors, Artists
& Ministries: Hardbacks, Paperbacks, eBooks, Audiobooks, Music,
Screenplays & Curricula

TINY GOD SYNDROME

ISBN: 978-1-61314-746-7

Cover Design & Interior Layout: Innovo Publishing, LLC

Printed in the United States of America
U.S. Printing History
First Edition: 2021

"He must increase, but I must decrease" (John 3:30).

CONTENTS

ACKNOWLEDGMENTS

I never thought I'd write a book. To be honest, I would have never dreamed of it. However, my accomplishments and dreams are not my own. They are a reflection of the man I have become due to the surrounding environment. People do not become great by themselves; rather, people become great when they surround themselves with greater people.

Throughout my life, I have been blessed to have met many different people—people who were encouraging, brave, and loving, along with those who were belittling, cowardice, and indifferent. Both the good and the bad served a purpose in my life. They taught me what it means to believe in something. They showed me that even the best of us fail. They always informed me of the dangers within this world, even if some of them were those very same dangers. Yes, people are capable of their own decisions and thoughts. (This is why we don't always blame the parents when a kid does something stupid in school. Everyone's bound to run into stupid at some point in their life . . . it's just a matter of who, what, and where.) However, we are a major reflection of the external acting on the internal. Our minds are molded by the world around us. Thus, our greatest feats are platformed upon those who shaped us.

I have several people I would like to thank for not only this book but all of my accomplishments within the last four years:

To my parents: Thank you for always pushing me. There have been numerous occasions where I have wanted to give up, but you have told me to never leave a task unfinished. Despite my complaining and foolish behavior, you have loved me more than I could possibly understand. Mom, you have always made sure I was well fed and safe. You always beared a great load so that I could do things that most kids couldn't. You are a rock that stabilizes the family. Without you, there would be utter chaos. Without your hard work, I would not be who I am today. Dad, thank you for all of the wisdom you have instilled in me. Life lessons and stern talks were a frequent thing growing up, and I appreciate that. You never hesitated to tell me what I was good at and encourage me in those areas. However, this encouragement was not full of smoke but real as I saw success in these areas more than others. You've helped keep me in line by disciplining me when necessary and forgiving me when I just needed to be calmed down. Throughout the years, both of you have sacrificed time, money, and sleep on my behalf, and for that I am grateful.

To my sister and brother-in-law: Thank you for always being there. I'm glad I have someone close enough that I can talk with when I need to. You'd do anything for me, and I can come to y'all with questions and stories that I might not tell Mom or Dad. You've been good friends, and I can't wait to see what an amazing daughter y'all will raise.

To my friends: Thank you for staying close. We've created so many great memories. We've laughed together and cried together, and through it all, we have been there for each other. I have been blessed to have as many friends that I have had. These friends are of course true friends that really mean something. You all have made me a better person by being great people. Everyone has been encouraging and loving through thick and thin, and for that I am grateful.

To my teachers: Thank you for being my mentors. At my school, I was lucky enough to have teachers that were intentional both inside and outside the classroom. You helped me persevere and constantly checked up on me throughout the years to see how I was doing. I would not be the person I am today without you.

To others: If you have coached me or taught me or done any kind of mentoring in my life, you have influenced me in some way. Although I wish I could mention everyone by name, the thank yous might be bigger than the book itself. Therefore, I would just like to say, you know who you are. You have made a greater impact on my life than you could ever know.

Thank you, everyone,

Jake Walker

1
THE TRAIN

The clanging of pots and pans echoed throughout the hostel's open rooms. The empty rooms, however, were deathly silent. Everyone had left to go down to the river, and those who stayed behind were either napping or taking showers. I, on the other hand, eagerly awaited dinner as I sat on the third floor of the balcony in a plastic chair that nearly split in two every time I sat down—but taking the risk of breaking the chair and busting my rear was worth it, for I had just spent the last four hours destroying a concrete foundation with a sledgehammer. If I were to fall, I figured that the cement ground shaded by the tin roof that often roared with the rain would keep me cool. Fortunately, the chair was stable, and I was able to prop my feet up on the railing of the balcony and take a deep breath of relief.

I turned to my right and reached for the guitar I had swiped from the girl who had been leading us in worship. The guitar was new, and the strings were heavenly. Surprisingly, even with the intense humidity, none of them were even out of tune. I strummed away with no care in the world, except for the thought of what might be our evening meal.

I took notice of the scenery set before me. A sun that radiated bright, with auburn and violet accents and pink undertones—merging with the tree line of the Amazonian rainforest. The falling sun made the green trees dark and hard to make out, yet it illuminated its colors throughout the rolling sky.

Suddenly, a feeling overcame me. It was a feeling such as joy, contentment, comfort, and peace. Where did this come from? Why did I all of a sudden have this feeling? I am by no means a "sensitive" guy . . . so, why? Why now? Why me? It was by no means the music I had been playing (I am what the average call "mediocre" at guitar). I don't believe it to be my stomach either (I was hungry, but hunger irritates me; it does not make me emotional). Whatever it was, it was breaking me down yet simultaneously building me up.

At this point, I was on the verge of tears. *This is ridiculous!* I thought to myself as I suppressed even the idea of letting a tear fall from my eye onto the guitar below. Two hours ago I was sledgehammering away, drenched with sweat, discussing college football; I couldn't have felt more manly in that moment. So why on earth was I on the verge of tears just a few hours later?

Throughout the course of the week, several people had given devotionals either at breakfast or dinner. Later that evening, I heard a devotional from one of the members on the mission team. Although they spoke with enthusiasm, I found it difficult to pay attention. I'm sure there was no lack of importance in the message, but rather it was my own fault. I was still stuck on the fact that I almost cried over a sunset, and I was still amazed at the fact that I couldn't get over it. I have nothing against sunsets, except when they stir emotion inside me.

Looking around, not truly focused on the Word being taught, I noticed something taped to the side of a cooler. My eyes latched onto it, as I thought about what it was. *Oh, the devo signup—that's what it is*, I said to myself. I then tried to move my eyes away from the sheet, but my mind stayed focused on the list of names. For some reason, I had the urge to give a devotional. This urge baffled me because I knew that I had a fear of public speaking. Even worse, I didn't have to be speaking to be nervous; if I was in front of people in general, I was immediately consumed by the heavy pit lodged in my stomach.

What was I to talk about anyway? The sunset that somehow touched my spirit? "Oh, I was just overwhelmed by how beautiful the sunset was . . . it just melted my soul. And I thought to myself, *This must be what heaven's like*." Absolutely not! That'd be ridiculous. However, I felt the need to do a devotional because our motto for the trip was getting comfortable with being uncomfortable (stepping outside your comfort zone). So if not the sunset, then what could I do?

That night I went to bed thinking about two things: what will I talk about tomorrow, and why am I still hung up on this sunset?

Every morning at breakfast, Jason Ellis, one of the leaders for the Ecuador trip, would give out handwritten letters from our friends and family. The letters usually contained, "I'm praying for you . . . this trip will be life changing . . ." or an inspirational Bible verse. (All of the letters I received were special, and I want to thank all who took the time to sit down and hand write me personalized words of encouragement while I was away.)

As I rifled through my letters, I came across one from my youth minister, Kyle Jacobson. The opening line was, "Read Isaiah 6 . . . I'll wait." So I put away my plate from breakfast and pulled up the ESV app on my phone, then began to read.

In the year that King Uzziah died, I saw the Lord, high and exalted, seated on a throne; and the train *of his robe filled the temple. ² Above him were seraphim, each with six wings: With two wings they covered their faces, with two they covered their feet, and with two they were flying. ³ And they were calling to one another:*

"Holy, holy, holy is the Lord Almighty;
the whole earth is full of his glory."

⁴ At the sound of their voices the doorposts and thresholds shook and the temple was filled with smoke.

⁵ "Woe to me!" I cried. "I am ruined! For I am a man of unclean lips, and I live among a people of unclean lips, and my eyes have seen the King, the Lord Almighty."

⁶ Then one of the seraphim flew to me with a live coal in his hand, which he had taken with tongs from the altar. ⁷ With it he touched my mouth and said, "See, this has touched your lips; your guilt is taken away and your sin atoned for."

⁸ Then I heard the voice of the Lord saying, "Whom shall I send? And who will go for us?"

And I said, "Here am I. Send me!"

I looked through Isaiah 6 and then went back to the letter to find what Kyle had written. Kyle went on to describe the Seraphim, saying, "God designs creatures to dwell in their habitat. Birds have wings and light bone structure for flight. Fish have gills in order to breathe underwater. These Seraphim were created in the presence of God. These perfect, holy beings need wings to cover their face . . . because God is that radiant." As soon as I read that, I knew what I wanted to talk about. I wanted to proclaim the holiness of God. I felt it was something that most people often get wrong or underestimate, so it would be good to talk about—not because I thought I could do a good job but because everyone falls short in describing how *holy* God is.

Throughout the course of the day, I reread Isaiah several times, each time finding something new to talk about. Yet I struggled to find the right words to fit into my fifteen-minute time slot.

Dinner neared, and I reviewed my notes as much as possible before dinner started. When dinner was served, I probably only ate four bites of chicken and shuffled around whatever vegetable was on my plate that night. Also, my leg decided to twitch uncontrollably, increasing with speed as dinner went on, just like a bomb ticks faster and faster as it reaches detonation. I needed to calm down. *It's only a quick devotional*, I thought to myself. *Anything I say, no one will even remember in two days.*

Surprisingly, the words *no one cares* did not seem to calm me down before I spoke. Nevertheless, the time had come for me to give my devotion. I stood up in between the two large wooden tables where we ate and grabbed my Bible propped against the large support beam that held the tin roof above. I looked at every face that looked right back at mine, and then, after a brief hesitation, I began to speak.

To start out, as any devotional usually does, I read the verses of scripture. Although it was probably the twenty-third time I read it, the words convicted me like they hadn't before. It was not that the scripture did not make sense beforehand; rather, it was that I did not realize the practical application to my own life. I kept on reading, and my mind hung on one verse in particular—verse 1: "The train of his robe filled the temple." I continued to mindlessly read the rest of the verses, but my focus was not on anything but those eight words. Like a slap across the face, it was clear the intent of the words. Quickly, I broke down this short statement into two parts.

Part 1: "the train of his robe." I recalled from various history classes and movies that a robe, at least the robe talked about here, was a king's robe. The robe always had a train that is similar to the train of a bride's dress. The train was a representation of three main things: power, glory, and righteousness. The longer the train of a bride, the more status and nobility she held. The longer the train of a king, the more might and honor he had.

Part 2: "filled the temple." Oh, the awe and splendor that is held in the train of a king. Yet no king's robe can encompass their whole palace. No matter how great they might be in the eyes of man, they are but a speck to the God we call Yahweh. For we know that His robe fills the whole temple.

When I read this and truly understood in my heart what it was saying, I was then able to attempt to fathom God's holiness (Ecclesiastes 3:11). Still, no one can ever truly understand the extent to which a *holy* King's power resides. Yet after hearing it out loud and reading it for the twenty-third time that day, I quivered ever so slightly. I shook not for the light breeze that may have caught the July air, or for the fact that I missed something crucial inside Isaiah 6. No, it was as if a doctor had walked in and given me the test results to a horrid cancer. This disease was violent, rampant, and invisible to the naked eye. Every hour spent with the disease slowly kills you, and to not catch it immediately is to your demise. The longer the disease sits, the more it will metastasize; yet the longer it sits, the more invisible it will become. If you allow it, this disease will be the downfall of every last thing you do.

I thank God that He handed me the test results that revealed to me my disease. For if I had not heard the dreaded news that I was infected, then I would have surely suffered at the hands of my own ignorance. I had TGS (*Tiny God Syndrome*) and was in desperate need of a cure.

I write these things not to scare you but to warn you. To warn you of the wretched and vile thought that power resides in the hands of men; to tell you of the lies embedded in our minds and to show you that there is a cure. Believer or non-believer, do not be afraid, for this cure is covered by insurance. There is no co-pay, no follow-up appointment, and no extra work for you. All that is required is that you accept the cure.

2
THE SUNSET

R adiant colors filled the air as pink, orange, and violet rays crossed the seemingly endless skyline. Every color held unique beauty that words could not describe. I also took note of the trees and how they seemed to stretch for miles east to west. I could not deny the beauty that was set before my own eyes, yet it puzzled me how something so simple could overwhelm me in this way.

As I reflected on the sunset after my devotional, I thought critically about the vivid scenery still stuck in the back of my mind. Then I thought about what makes a sunset and how it scientifically works. In order to get colors such as orange and pink, you have to have the right wavelength. Also, the amount of pollution within the air can determine how vivid a sunset will be. Smog and other carbon emissions that settle at lower elevations tend to absorb large amounts of light. This scatters the wavelengths and makes it difficult to pick up on all the vivid colors of a sunset. Luckily, the village of Misahualli had not been industrialized, so carbon emissions were extremely low. Also, the altitude was high, resulting in an intense colorful phenomenon due to the lack of large air particles.

I began to think about the trees that were silhouetted by the illuminating sun. These trees were extremely large, with trunks that, on average, were eighty-two feet high. With that high of a trunk, the root system must be exceptionally profound. After examining the exterior of the tree, you must look at the complex interior. For example: the interconnected transportation system within the tree runs throughout and delivers nutrients necessary for the process of photosynthesis. This process in turn makes glucose that leads to pyruvate, which can release adenosine triphosphate (energy).

Now, you are probably saying one of two things: Why is this person ranting about how light works? What does this have to do with this book or Christianity? Well, I say none of this to brag about my seventh grade biology skills. Although I love biology and all science, I am no botanist or meteorologist. I am just a guy who happened to admire a sunset. That admiration led me to a thought of complexity and how things work. In fact, it helped me realize how intelligent of a Creator you need to have to get something so complex.

Another great example is the human body. Its complexity runs to places we still have not yet ventured. There are mysteries within our own physiology that God has yet to reveal to us.

I hope I am making myself clear when I say that you cannot have a small God when you look at your surrounding environment. Whether you read about quantum chemistry, look at how a muscle contracts, or even pause to admire a sunset, it is all complex and out of our control.

Next, I want to say that you must not—MUST NOT—begin to worship the creation over the Creator. Yes, the creation is beautiful, but how much more beauty is there in the mind and heart of the Creator? Oh, how brilliant, bold, and elegant the painting is, but how brilliant, bold, and elegant is the Artist behind the portrait itself? There is a fine line between admiration and worship, and I urge you to be careful to not get caught up in the beauty of creation but rather to submerge yourself in the God so beautiful to create it.

Why not get caught up in the creation?

Everything Is Meaningless

The words of the Teacher, son of David, king in Jerusalem:

"Meaningless! Meaningless!"
says the Teacher.
"Utterly meaningless!
Everything is meaningless."
What do people gain from all their labors
at which they toil under the sun?
Generations come and generations go,
but the earth remains forever.
The sun rises and the sun sets,
and hurries back to where it rises.
The wind blows to the south
and turns to the north;
round and round it goes,
ever returning on its course.
All streams flow into the sea,
yet the sea is never full.
To the place the streams come from,
there they return again.
All things are wearisome,
more than one can say.
The eye never has enough of seeing,
nor the ear its fill of hearing.
What has been will be again,
what has been done will be done again;
there is nothing new under the sun.
Is there anything of which one can say,
"Look! This is something new"?

It was here already, long ago;
It was here before our time.
No one remembers the former generations,
and even those yet to come
will not be remembered
by those who follow them.
(Ecclesiastes 1:1-11)

Our time on Earth is short. Yes, His creation is beautiful, but this is not our home. Do not forget that this is a broken place. You have been commanded to be in the world, not of it (John 17:14-19):

> *I have given them your word and the world has hated them, for they are not of the world any more than I am of the world. [15] My prayer is not that you take them out of the world but that you protect them from the evil one. [16] They are not of the world, even as I am not of it. [17] Sanctify them by the truth; your word is truth. [18] As you sent me into the world, I have sent them into the world. [19] For them I sanctify myself, that they too may be truly sanctified.*

We are called to be a guide to those who are lost, but do not take your eyes off of the cross. There are things in this world that are extremely attractive to the naked eye; however, nothing compares to the beauty that lies at Calvary. If you choose to stray from the Father, the world may welcome you with open arms. Although the embrace of the world may be soft and warm, the hands of the world will quickly grow calloused and bitter. For the world cannot love as God has loved.

A good friend of mine traveled to Las Vegas recently for vacation. Vegas wouldn't have been my first pick, but this guy is wilder than I am. Fortunately his trip went well, and he returned safely home to tell me all about it. He described the initial landing as he flew in at night:

Everything was lit up from the rooftops to the casinos. The colors were just as bright as anything you can imagine in a firework show. Soon after I landed and got checked into my hotel, I went to the bar. [I feel obliged to state my friend was of drinking age.] The hotel was nice enough to grant me some free beverages at the affiliated casino, where the bartender was pleased to serve me. As soon as I walked into the gambling hall, I felt like a high roller. My wallet was feeling hot, and my ego was feeling lucky. I gambled for a while, and to my liking, I was winning a lot! At the rate I was going, I expected to completely earn back the money I lost on the trip and then some.

After a few days, my hot streak began to wear off. What I thought would be black turned out red, and what I counted as twenty-one somehow added to twenty-four. I soon lost all that I had once earned in the beginning. At this point in the trip, it was time to go. I had lost big and was in no condition to keep on visiting the ATM. The great light show put on by the casino had lost its effect, and the bartender seemed less eager to serve me as I went from whiskeys to Bud Lights.

Vegas is a perfect example of that which is fleeting. The welcome is warm, and the initial high is indescribable. However, this world is not your friend. The indulgence will leave you vacant and lost, forever searching for the high that once was but never again will be. Even if you obtain the once great high to its full capacity, it will never be enough to satisfy the longing desire of fulfillment inside the heart of man. Therefore, do not search for salvation in those who cannot provide it; rather, look toward the cross. Jesus is the ultimate provider of the satisfaction you've been longing for. Unlike the bartender, Jesus' tap never runs dry and is always free. He [Jesus] has been longing for you to go back home . . . to your true home.

God also created work for mankind. Hard work is in no way a bad thing, but do not let your god be success. Measuring yourself by your accomplishments will always leave you wanting more. After Super Bowl XXXIX (39), Tom Brady had won three Super Bowls and at age twenty-seven had accomplished more than most NFL quarterbacks will achieve in their lifetime. All this said, Brady debuted in a *60 Minute* interview with Steve Kroft after winning his third Super Bowl in only five seasons with the Patriots. Brady went on to say in the interview, "Why do I have three Super Bowl rings and still think there is something greater out there for me? There has to be more than this. What else is there for me?"

There is a hard truth that sometimes hard work does not pay off to the extent we want it to. To seek fulfillment in personal achievements is foolish, but to seek purpose in something that's everlasting is wise.

SALT WATER. Picture this, you are stranded on a raft in the middle of the Atlantic Ocean. The sun is brutally beating down on your already blistered skin. You struggle to keep your eyes open as the sun produces an intense reflection off the water. Dehydration settles in, and you have barely enough strength to stagger to your knees. You look down at the ocean and fall to your chest, head over the raft, drinking the salt water. It's refreshing for about ten minutes, but due to the high concentration of salt, your mouth turns dry.

You lean over the raft again and drink more. This time only five minutes pass before your mouth is completely dry and you crave more. Eventually, you find yourself neck deep, guzzling the very thing that is drying your mouth out, leaving you wanting more. Finally, you come up for air, and to your surprise, a fisherman finds you and maneuvers toward you. He stops his boat about ten yards from your slowly sinking raft. The fisherman looks at you and yells, "Climb on, I'll take you to shore. You are only twenty-eight miles from the coast. I can get you water—purified water that won't make you sick. I have fruit that has been in a cooler that even refreshes the eyes when you look upon it. I can give you shelter, a place to hide out from the near approaching storm. Please come aboard."

You look back at the fisherman and see him leaning over the rail near his ladder, tossing you the life preserver. You stare at the life preserver—it's within arm's reach. Freedom has never felt so close. You begin to reach out your hand, and just as your fingers hover above the tightly wound rope, you look back up at the fisherman and say, "I don't need saving. The salt water will be my refreshment, my torn shirt shall be my shelter, and the fish will be my nourishment if I am lucky."

Often times we drink the salt water of this world. Whether that water be money, sex, social status, or anything that is apart from Christ—we are left wanting more. Yes! Salt water will only leave you wanting more! People often say, "It looks so refreshing; it looks so good; it's pleasing to think about; I just wish I could go back to the thing that made me feel good." Let me rephrase that: "Let me go back to the thing that was killing me, because in my heart I believe I can sustain myself—because in my mind God isn't good enough for me. The fisherman that was willing to save me wasn't offering what I truly desire."

The water offered by the fisherman is sustaining. The water will satisfy the longing desire that so many of us seek in this world. If you refuse the water, then we have one of two problems:

1. You believe your way is better, and because of that, you live in an egotistical manner. You are self-righteous, and self-righteousness is not an easy way

to live. It requires you to always look your best. You will be required to constantly be in competition with your peers and draw comparisons between you and others. There is nothing wrong with striving to be the best, but it's the *reason why* you strive. If you are trying to prove that you're better than someone else, then it's self-righteousness. If you are attempting to be the best in order to better yourself and the people around you, I would not label this a self-righteous act. However, do not look upon those who you consider less and grow pride in your heart, less you want to be seen as a pharisee by God—the very people who believed they were better than the Son of Man. God Almighty died for the drunkard and the prostitute and *you*. Friend, remember that you were so broken that the God of the universe had to die for you. Remind yourself that the payment for the drunkard's sin was the death of Christ, and the payment for the sins of the prostitute was the death of Christ, and the payment for *your* sins was the death of Christ (Romans 3:23, "For all have sinned and fall short of the glory of God"). At Calvary, we are all made equal. No man is better than anyone else. Therefore, the Cross is the greatest equalizer.

2. You are not willing to give up the salt water. Often, people are scared of the extremity of Christianity. No, Christianity is not a works-based religion; in fact, I would argue that it isn't a religion at all (everything classified as a "religion" requires works, but Christianity is the only "religion" that requires your faith alone). But in order to follow Jesus, you need to be prepared to give up your worldly desires (Matthew 19:21, "Jesus answered, 'If you want to

be perfect, go, sell your possessions and give to the poor, and you will have treasure in heaven. Then come, follow me'"). Friend, what are you clinging to? What are you unwilling to give up? Surely the salt water you abide in is not so refreshing that it satisfies you completely. Who is your God? Is it your greed and lust of monetary wealth? Or perhaps your work that seems to only drive a wedge between your marriage and/or children? What are you gluttonizing? What is more important than the God of the universe? You can attempt to argue that the salt water is refreshing, but for how long? (1 John 2:17, "And the world is passing away along with its desires, but whoever does the will of God abides forever"). Do you not know that the things of this world will pass away, but the living God is eternal? Yes, I realize that was an extreme example, but any idol, no matter how small, cannot and must not enter the life of man.

This does not get at the heart of the issue. There is something greater that underlies the heart of those who refuse the water of the fisherman. They refuse the water because they do not know the Man who offers it. They refuse the salvation because they do not know the God who offers it. Yes, they are chained to their oppressive sin not because they refuse to leave but because they do not understand how to escape. Do you not see that the reason people go on sinning is because, in their eyes, sin is bigger and better than God? Understanding the complexity and beauty in a loving yet just God has become hard to do. Why? Our culture has either a misconstrued definition of love or a self-contrived version of justice; and if we somehow are lucky enough to understand justice and love, it's hard and unlikely that we enforce both of them at the same time very well.

There is only one true model from which we get perfect love and justice. *Perfect love* is to sacrifice everything for the benefit of nothing. *Perfect justice* is the punishment of those who have committed heinous acts against that which is purely innocent. The only place where both of these work together in complete unity is at Calvary. Although we were an enemy of God because of our impurity and sinfulness, we have been spared from the wrath of the Father. However, someone must satisfy the wrath of God and take on the penalty of our sins. Jesus, fully man and fully God, the perfect Messiah, stepped in as the great Intercessor and through Him expressed the perfect example of love, while experiencing perfect justice.

Now, what about after you get on the boat? Imagine that you clasp the life preserver and climb aboard the fisherman's boat. You have been saved and are looking forward to an everlasting paradise that is found at shore. However, your storms do not cease just yet, and your seas are not always calm. For some, your seas seem to unceasingly rage. Do not turn to God and say, *Why am I still suffering?* For you were not promised tranquility on this side of heaven. Rather, look to the day when you will suffer no more. Keep your eyes set on the shore; take them off of the raging seas. For you have been promised eternal paradise with the One who saved you.

Also, it is important to remember that once you are on the boat, you cannot fall off. There is no "man overboard" when it comes to Christ. Your salvation is secure and guaranteed once you have accepted Him. No matter how bad the troubled waters are, they will not last forever, nor will they harm the boat.

Finally, remember that you do not have to steer the boat. You are not the captain of your life anymore; you do not have to navigate the uneasy waters alone. Your God is in charge of your life, and He will deliver you to life everlasting. For He is the best navigator to ever be and will surely deliver you in the days to come.

3

THE CHIHUAHUA

I t was the beginning of fall. The leaves on the trees were changing, and the temperature had subdued to a cool sixty degrees. My mother and I took our three dogs to the dog park to let them run around and expend as much energy as possible. We arrived, and to my surprise, there were lots of dogs there, each running around and having a good time. I also noticed the diversity in dogs. There were large dogs, small dogs, fluffy dogs, and short-haired dogs. All the dogs were different sizes, shapes, and colors. They all ran around, barking and playfully jumping into each other. But to my surprise, the loudest, most obnoxious dog there was not the Great Dane, not the Golden Retriever, or even the stocky Bulldog. No, the most outrageous dog there was the Chihuahua. The Chihuahua would search the premises for the largest dog out there, then proceed to bark incessantly at him till he or she would play with him. If the Chihuahua was ignored, then he or she would pick a fight with the clearly bigger dog. Before the Chihuahua was eaten alive, the owner came and scooped him up. The Chihuahua proceeded to bark repeatedly, and in a comical image, I thought about Scrappy from Scooby-Doo saying, "Let me at 'em."

I used the analogy of Scrappy the dog because we often think we are bigger than we are. We are the Chihuahua and ultimately have a big opinion of ourselves. The bigger we become in our minds, the smaller God becomes. We are accomplishing just the opposite of what John writes in John 3:30: "Lord Jesus I must decrease, so that you can increase." Egocentrism is one of the detrimental causes of *Tiny God Syndrome*. In egocentrism, you are the center: all you can see is yourself. There is no room for God at the center of your world because you are god. It is a very dangerous thing to hold yourself in high regard. If you have an egocentric mindset, then you will always be let down.

As humans, we are prone to constant error. Whatever mistakes we make affect the people around us and ourselves. And many of us who have an egocentric worldview are blinded to our own error by pride. It is in our pride that we lose the sense of who God is. Pride does not always stem from rejection of God but from ignorance of how great God truly is.

Often our high opinion of ourselves sets us up for failure . . . or even worse, destruction. Like the Chihuahua going against the Great Dane, we would be obliterated by life. Quickly put in our place as merely mortal men with very little control over our future. We cannot defeat the Great Danes in our life, or at least not alone.

In the story of David and Goliath, the Israelites are battling a great army called the Philistines. Both armies are camped across from one another with a valley in between them. Every morning, a man named Goliath would arise from the Philistine camp and go down into the valley. Goliath was the mightiest warrior of the Philistines. The Bible describes his appearance as such: The messianic text records Goliath's height of six cubits in a span, which translates to about nine feet six inches. In addition to a detailed description of his stature, the Bible also appeals to the armor of Goliath. He had a bronze helmet weighing about thirty pounds, a bronze coat of mail carrying about five thousand shekels (about one hundred fifty pounds), and a spear that in total weighed about fifty pounds. It can be assumed that by this description, Goliath was by no means a small man. Also, being raised in a war-like environment, Goliath had most likely been trained to fight ever since he could walk—therefore, making Goliath an intimidating warrior to anyone.

Then the Bible describes the three ways Goliath threatens the Israelites. *Theologically*, he says that the Israelites will become servants to the Philistines and their gods. *Socially*, he demoralizes Saul, the leader of the Israelites. *Militarily*, he reduces the fight to a one-on-one combat and proceeds to make fun of the only challenger who will step forward (David).

Even the mightiest of warriors in the Israelite camp would cower in fear when they saw Goliath. Most would say, "Of course we cannot win against a warrior like Goliath." Yet a teenage shepherd boy who had no armor or military decoration, let alone experience, was ready to go against one of the mightiest warriors in the world. Despite the size of the enemy and the ill war experience David has, he chooses to fight when everyone else runs.

In 1 Samuel 17:34, David exclaims, "The LORD who delivered me from the paw of the lion and from the paw of the bear will deliver me from the hand of this Philistine." David, with confidence, goes against Goliath, who in his eyes was just another beast of the fields that would easily perish at the mighty strength of the Lord.

Friend, we must remember that this is not a story to inspire us to go out and slay all the Goliaths in our life. For us, it is a picture of what Christ has already done for us! Your victory is in the Lord. Humbly, God came as the Perfect

David to defeat death and save us from our sins. One on one, Christ versus death, where Christ came to conquer so that death would swiftly die. We should not mix this up as a story to predominantly proclaim our own power, for we have no power apart from the Lord. So do not grow prideful nor arrogant in the Lord's power within you, but remain humble, knowing that it is not your own power. On the other hand, do not be so cowardly that you forget who is on your team. Stand for the Lord in the midst of adversity, for He has already won. The victory is yours in Christ. Therefore do not let your knees grow weak nor your lips grow tired, but stand firm in the salvation that is your God and proclaim the holy victory of the One most high.

It is interesting to find that when the Philistines took the Ark of the Covenant from Ebenezer to Ashdod, they placed it in their temple with their god, Dagon. When the people of Ashdod arose the next morning, they found that Dagon had fallen face forward before the Ark of God. So they propped up Dagon and placed him beside the Ark of God again. The following day, they came into the temple to find Dagon lying face first, decapitated with his hands cut from him (1 Samuel 5). There is no god nor man who will stand right before the Lord, the El Shaddai (the Great Almighty). He is the only God, for He is Yahweh (the Great I AM).

So when you look back at the story of David and Goliath, you see a God big enough to save a people group not big enough to save themselves. David intercedes for the Israelites, just as the God of the universe intercedes for us through His perfect Son, Jesus Christ.

Lastly, David takes the sword of Goliath and decapitates him, exposing him as weak and ill-favored in the eyes of the Lord—again creating a picture that ultimately evil destroys itself, for it was with the very sword that Goliath planned to do harm that ended up killing him. All of this parallels the story of Dagon and the Ark of God, where God brings forth justice to those who threaten His people and in the end favors those who trust in Him. Therefore, do not boast about yourself as a man big enough to slay his demons, but rejoice in a God who has slayed them for you. And do not cower, for the Lord your God has victory and will complete that victory in the days to come.

As soon as we make God smaller, we then downplay His divine law written on our heart. Our actions become less offensive in our eyes because we no longer are judged on the basis of a holy, perfect, just God, but rather by our own judgement, which is often extremely flawed. Although it is often not hard to self-criticize, it is difficult to self-examine. For example, when I was younger, the TV shows I often watched would affect my attitude toward my parents and others. I would pick up on specific character traits of actors on the shows and then become that person. However, I was blinded to the fact that this was happening until my parents would mention it to me. It was only until someone else took notice of my actions and spoke up that I truly saw what I was doing.

Although we have people in our lives who can point out our sin that we may not have noticed, we cannot solely rely upon others to be the judge of our sins. This is because people are sinful and like to make light of their sin. They can easily say, "Well what you did isn't that bad." The only reason they would say this is because they wish to make light of their own sin and are coming from a worldly perspective.

Overall, however, we must not view sin as just an offense to fellow man. If we only view sin as an offense to man, then we will still not understand the full weight of our sin. Man is sinful and unrighteous and therefore does not always deserve or demand justice. For example, if we hear of a man who beats his wife or girlfriend and is shot in a separate incident completely unrelated to the physical abuse of a significant other, then we make an excuse, saying, "Oh, he had it coming or deserved it in some way." Although that may be true that he deserves punishment, we make light of the sin of the shooter who killed a random man in the street. What if the man he shot was a loving husband and father of two beautiful children? Do we now punish the sin differently for the shooter who had no knowledge of who the man was? Absolutely not . . . or at least we shouldn't. He has taken the life of a human being without the intent of seeking justice but rather for the pure desire to take the life of another. However, man's view and knowledge only extends so far. We can never truly know the motives of the shooter if he or she does not tell us. Consequently, the best judge of sin would be someone who was omnipotent (all knowing). That person could truly examine the heart of the killer and know if he murdered to carry out some sort of justice or only did so for purely evil motives.

With that said, we must understand God's omnipotence and ability to judge right from wrong in ways that our mortal minds cannot comprehend.

Francis Chan once used this analogy when on a beach. He didn't say anything at first and proceeded to grab a two-liter empty Coke bottle. Then he walked into the ocean and bent down and submerged the Coke bottle fully into the water. Once the bottle was completely full, he came back to his congregation and said, "The bottle is your mind, and the ocean is the knowledge of God." Therefore, we do not understand the mind of God, because it is so far beyond our comprehension. If the God of the universe is truly all knowing, and knowledge is infinite, then the mind of God must be infinite as well. So, friend, I hope you get the message when I say that the greatest, most just, perfect judge of the universe is God and no one else.

Not only is God omnipotent, but He is perfect in every way. The God of the universe is a holy God and cannot associate with that which is unholy. When we stop looking at our sin as an offense toward man and start looking at it as an offense toward God, the bar is certainly raised. We are held to exceptionally higher standards. We are demanded to be perfect, and even the slightest mess-up would be punishable by death and unacceptable to a God who is holy. Thus the sin of man is greater than first perceived. For we are not just harming the creation but the Creator. Take stealing a piece of candy, for example. Most would say that the petty theft is incomparable to a more destructive sin. Who are we to weigh the egregiousness of our sin when we do not take into account the righteousness of the One whom we sin against? To steal a piece of candy is to knowingly defy God and His law. For everyone knows the law of God and can give a general understanding of right vs. wrong (Romans 2:15). Therefore a man knows in his heart that he is openly going against what is right and accepting his sinful nature. To openly accept a sinful nature is to place yourself into a position above God. This is because you view God's law and He Himself as less important or less in charge than yourself and your own desires.

No one can completely rid themselves of sin. The only one who can wash away the guilty soul of man is Jesus. However, we can actively try to find ways to strip ourselves of sinful tendencies and kill the root of our thoughts that contribute to our actions. One way we can better assess our sinful thoughts that might lead to action is to look at who is being affected by our sin. First and foremost, look to God. Yes, you sin against man and can harm yourself by sinning, but the Lord had to bear the true weight of your sin more than you could ever know. Look to the cross: He bears the sin of the man who shot another human in cold blood just the same as He bears the sin of a child who decided to steal a piece of candy one afternoon. We must look at who we are truly offending and who ultimately is paying the cost.

4

THE ANXIETY

The following testimonies were provided to me via my peers. These are real stories, real people, and real problems facing my generation.

> *I thought my life was over for a long time when I heard the news that I had not gotten into the college I wanted. All that hard work, all those late nights staying up studying, neglecting time with friends in order to write college essays—because of my fixated mind. I refused most nights to even eat dinner with my family out of fear of not getting enough work done . . . or worse, having a brilliant idea for an essay and it slipping before I could get to my laptop and jot it down.*

***

> *One day back in February, I had had a pretty average day . . . nothing too bad. But on my way home, I got overwhelmed with the anxiety and sadness I had*

been ignoring. My parents weren't home, so I went straight to my room. I was shaking, and I couldn't breathe or walk, so I collapsed on the ground. I laid there and cried for about an hour. I've dealt with depression and anxiety for most of my life, so I've become accustomed to living in the moment, tossing a smile on, and not letting it affect me every hour of every day. Yes, I was still able to go out and see my friends and have happy times, but I do admit I am not the same person.

***

I latched on to the side of the toilet as tears streamed down my face and into my mouth and onto the seat. I laid there, aggressively throwing up and shaking out of fear of what people might think of me. It was anxiety. A severe case of anxiety that had not subdued for quite some time. For the next several days, I did not sleep nor did I eat, knowing that the only outcome would just be more vomiting. When would the pain stop? When would it end?

In a case study put on by the American Psychological Association, it was found that the average child today experiences the same level of anxiety as a psychiatric patient in the 1950s.[1] Furthermore, the CDC found that from 2007 to 2017, the suicide rate had risen in those ten to twenty-four years of age by an overwhelming 56%.[2] That would make suicide the second-leading cause of death of generation Z. These statistics are horrifyingly heartbreaking. They all raise brows and must be addressed in some way.

So my question is, *Why?* Why is it that the generation of today (Gen Z) seems to be filled with overwhelming amounts of anxiety? How come there's an idea that it all comes down to a few big decisions, and somehow those decisions define who you will always be? We can tell ourselves that we don't believe a few decisions dictate our final outcome; however, when placed into the moment, it's a trap many of us fall into, and you can easily find yourself believing the lie that X, Y, or Z is the determinant of your whole future.

There's three distinct reasons why I think this is happening. These are by no means the only reasons, just the ones I seem to find most common:

1. *The opportunity:* It's as if every bit of information known or capable of being known is readily available from the few simple taps of our fingers and an insertion into a search bar. If you want to know something, you can figure it out. Whether that be simple information about who won the thirty-first Super Bowl or maybe something more complex like how anaerobic respiration works. Radically different questions, but both extremely accessible answers.

   With all of the information available and the ever-growing knowledge in the world, students are expected to learn at an exceptionally faster rate than ever before. For example, my biology teacher once said that the chapter she had on cells was only two pages, because that's all they knew about cells back then. In today's society, you can find thousands of books that highlight so many different types of cells and their functions. Because science and math and all other realms of academics have made so many breakthroughs in recent years, it stresses the importance of retaining more and more information at a younger age. This expansion of new technology and knowledge expands the job market and creates more opportunities for the younger generation. Nevertheless, with a greater opportunity comes more responsibility to learn these skills at a younger age.

When pondering the thought of anxiety and why the generation of today would be more anxious, I remembered one thing my father said to me:

> *I never had as many opportunities as you did, but more opportunity means more freedom, and more freedom means more responsibility, and more responsibility means more pressure, and more pressure means more stress, and more stress means more anxiety. Therefore, the kids of today would definitely have more anxiety because of the pressure put on them and the higher expectations demanded from them. When I was young, if you went to college, that was great, but you only had two options pretty much growing up in Jackson, Mississippi. That was Mississippi State or Ole Miss. Then after you went to college, you'd come back home and marry the girl from high school you knew and work in town.*

Our current generation has several options, and my class alone of 143 students will be attending over forty different collegiate universities in more than fifteen states. This is a testament to the overwhelming amount of opportunities and stress put on them, with various scholarships and necessary ACT scores to get into said colleges. Kids of today will kill themselves by sacrificing mental, social, and physical health just to get into a particular university or get an extra two thousand dollars a year. This was not something the generation of our parents had to deal with—as my father also told me his first college tuition for a full semester was one hundred dollars. Yes, the academics, the infrastructure, and the amount of people attending college have all increased, which are all great things . . . but they all contribute to the overwhelming nature of *more*.

2. *The hypothetical:* If you look at the ACT, particularly the reading portion, you will find that some questions are strictly fact based (the answers can be found directly in the text), and others are inference based (and require you to make hypotheticals derived from the text). Now hold with me . . . ACT scoring has dramatically changed in the last fifty years. There has been a steady increase in the composite scoring over the last fifty years. However, this does not say that people of today are just naturally smarter or more gifted; rather, it shows how the style of thinking has changed and cognitive demand has increased. It would simply be chronological snobbery to suppose every generation is getting smarter than the one before and therefore is better overall.

A man by the name of James Flynn wrote a book and gave a TED talk answering the question, "Are people getting smarter?"[3] In short, Flynn concluded "no," but they have had to change the way they are thinking in today's environment. Yes, cognitive demands have increased, but what has really changed is the approach to which we answer questions. As a whole, society began to ask, *Why?* and *How?* And more importantly, *What if?* From these questions sparked a revolution of hypothetical questioning that led to a dramatic influx of people thinking more abstractly. A change in the style of thinking will mold the mind and not just affect the way you approach school but all situations in life.

The younger generations, millennials and even more so Gen Z, have been stressed into this hypothetical approach to thinking. This is why the test scores in these hypothetical-type questions have increased. The kids of today are not so much focused on the black and white but rather on the abstract grey. This of course shifts the psychological mindset, further contributing to the hypothetical mindset that older generations find hard to relate to. Yes, the "what if" mindset has contributed to the overall testing abilities and cognitive demand abilities of younger generations; yet an overall influx of anxiety has resulted in younger generations who are able to do this. Why? Simply because it has shifted the way one thinks about everyday situations. Thoughts such as, *What if I had gone to the party? What if I wore this instead? What if I did X, Y, or Z . . . would I be more liked? What if I hadn't done that, would people not like me or like me more? What if I could get this way or that way . . . would that help me in the long run?* All of these situations are traps we lay down for ourselves in order to create an ideal situation for our lives; however, most of these situations are unrealistic and are unachievable, and, in the end, they don't have the significant impact we think they have on our lives.

Generation Z is the only generation that can say, "We never knew what it was like to not have an iPhone." There has never been a time in my life that social media didn't exist, where books weren't accessible on screens, and where knowledge wasn't gained by the touch of a finger.

3. *The media and technology:* Technology can be a blessing and a curse. So much can be true at once, and that's just what Dr. Tim Elmore had to say in his interview with Carey Nieuwhof: "Many adults can't

understand this angst, saying: 'What do they feel stressed about? This is the most convenient time in earth's history to be alive.' While that's true, Gen Z lives with a paradox. These kids' lives are both easier and harder. Life is easier and quicker to navigate technologically, but more difficult to navigate psychologically and emotionally."[4] Dr. Elmore is conveying that social media and technology has created accessibility and community but has also opened a gateway for dependency and anxiety. In that, quick available access to community is fantastic, but when that community becomes your identity, problems will arise.

Our generation is the first generation to always have social media. Therefore, we do not have the same escape that some may have had before us. FOMO (fear of missing out) was never a big deal until the twenty-first century. For example, in today's society, if you don't get invited to a party, you will quickly know you didn't get invited because someone will post a picture or video at the party after only being there for twenty minutes. However, in 1980, you had no way of knowing what was going on at the party, who all was there, and how long it lasted. Therefore, it was hard for people to develop FOMO in the twentieth century.

In today's standard, through use of every available social media platform, people can find out all of the preceding information in a matter of five seconds. With certain applications, the photo you take and post can also provide information on when the individual was last "online," who he or she was with, and what their exact location is. That's insane! Information that most people would have to figure out two weeks later can now be accessed and known in a matter of seconds. This constant access to media can spark the "what if" mindset that so many people have. And if we are not careful, the world of social media can quickly diverge into constant questioning and aspiration. The questioning is based upon the false portrayal that is often on display in so many people's social media feeds and stories. This not only leads to unrealistic expectations for our own life but also dissociation from those who are viewed as perfect— all of which creates a false narrative that states, *If I only had X, Y, or Z, I would be happy.*

This, of course, is the aspiration. In themselves, goals are not a bad thing. But the reason for the goal must not stem from an egocentric point of view. The goal cannot become one's identity, as it will only leave you empty, regardless of whether or not it is achieved.

There are those of us who rely on social media and other forms of technology as a release from the real world. As I took a poll from my high school (which I can only imagine to be very similar to every other high school), I found that upwards of 90% of students report using some form of social media before going to bed. Why? Although for most it might be a habit, I have to believe that others find it to be an escape. What do I mean? Isolation is a scary thing, and for all of the stress and anxiety built up in the lives of Gen Z, being alone with one's thoughts would have to be a literal nightmare. The ability to indulge in something that requires mindless interaction is very appealing to those who don't want to use their minds. I do not mean that in the sense that they are afraid of actually trying something; rather, they are scared of what rabbit holes they might follow if left isolated with nothing but their thoughts.

I also mentioned the people that have made it a habit to look at social media before bedtime. I would bet that most of them have become reliant on social media as necessary means to sleep. Just like any other thing when used in repetition, it can become addicting. Therefore, social media can act like a literal drug that one can become dependent upon for anxiety relief. This anxiety can stem from a multitude of reasons, some being fear of not being informed, fear of missing out, and even fear of thinking.

To fear thinking is something that has been instilled in us through social media. It used to be that people were forced to think when they were alone because they had nothing else to do; there was no such thing as social media or even smart phones for that matter. Every other generation has been forced to think when alone and was not offered an easy way out. Even in today's society, if you see someone in a waiting room, standing in line, or even out at dinner, they are on their phones. Technology has created a dependency upon distraction within our culture. This of course can lead to the extreme of early generations finding it difficult to formulate their own opinions. Many people today will read something online or hear something on the news and immediately take it as fact. Regardless of your political views, we can all agree that every media outlet has their biases. However, it wasn't until the seventies that news outlets began to be opinionated. Beforehand, the FCC made all broadcasting as unbiased as possible. Radically different in today's society, every media outlet has an opinion on everything. It's great to hear someone argue for what they believe in, but it's dangerous in the fact that we no longer have to formulate our own opinions as we let major media outlets formulate them for us. This in turn contributes to the lack of critical thinking required from Generation Z—this all furthering the neglect of isolated thoughts in our culture.

Our generation also lacks those who can think critically. The inability to challenge oneself in thought will lead to a weak ability to make big decisions. Why is this the case? Well, through technology, everything has become so much more accessible. If I sit down to read various thoughts from Socrates or Plato, I can just look up what they are saying in simpler terms in a matter of seconds. Another example is Shakespeare. When kids read Shakespeare today, they are not as challenged as they used to be. Technology has even given us a side-by-side translation that puts his words into modern terms you can understand. Don't get me wrong; I think this is an efficient tool, but unfortunately that does take away from the ability to challenge oneself. You might understand something faster, but the goal isn't just comprehension. The main goal is endurance and challenging oneself to critically think.

Technology has taken perseverance away from us, and with that, it has weakened our ability to make tough decisions. This innate ability to make tough decisions places stress upon kids when they have to step up and finally make those decisions. Obviously, this would cause anxiety in anyone.

So how can the anxieties of the world be solved with a big God? Well, imagine if you could rest in the fact that you didn't have complete control over your life. Most people would say, "What? I want to have control over my life. If only

I had that, then I'd be fine." However, I say that's *Tiny God Syndrome* and will only fail you in the end. Think about it: humans mess up and make mistakes all the time, but what if someone better than us were in control of our lives—someone who was omnipotent, omniscient, and omnipresent. That person would surely be better at controlling our future, having already known the future, right? Yes!

In John 13:33, when Jesus is talking to the disciples, He refers to them as "little children." Grown men are called little children—not just *children* but *little children*—in order to display a point of dependency on God. Jesus is saying, *You need me.* God is your dependency. It is not an insult but a comfort to be dependent upon a holy God. For there is no better security than Christ. We must not lean upon our own understanding but rather trust in the Lord with all our heart (Proverbs 3:5).

God knows your future, and His intended will for your life is good. Ultimately, God wants you to have restoration and live in eternal glory with Him in paradise. It should be comforting when we realize that we are not in complete control of our life because we often mess things up and make bad decisions. Therefore, we should take comfort in knowing that God will place us where He wants us, and all things work together for the good of those who believe in His name (Romans 8:28). No matter what you do, you cannot screw up the will of God.

Let me share this analogy that my dad told me. When you're a young child, you have people older than you and wiser than you who make decisions for you. You're not in complete control of your life, and thank goodness! If every child didn't have an adult helping them make decisions, then we would quickly have a generation of unhealthy, illiterate, miserable children. Is it not true that life's questions get more complicated as you grow older? Are we still not children in comparison to our God we call Father? Should we not be thankful and confident and restful, knowing that we have a God who is steering our lives for our benefit?

I am quickly reminded of Ruth while thinking about this form of rest. In the book of Ruth, we have three main characters: Naomi, Boaz, and, of course, Ruth. Naomi is the mother-in-law to Ruth, and both Naomi and Ruth are widows. Both of the women move back to Israel where Naomi is from. When they arrive and chapter 2 begins, Naomi and Ruth are both discussing how they will get food. Then Ruth says she will get something for them and goes into the fields of a man named Boaz. Boaz then grants provisions to Ruth and is very generous to her and her mother-in-law. Ruth goes home to Naomi and tells her about Boaz, and Naomi gets very excited and calls Boaz, "the family redeemer." The family redeemer was someone who would marry the widow and protect the family and provide for the family.

Chapter 3 now starts with Naomi dressing up Ruth in a way that shows her availability for marriage. Then Ruth leaves to go meet Boaz in the fields. When she arrives, she finds him sleeping and waits till he awakes. He wakes up, and she asks him to redeem her family and marry her. He admires her "noble character," and the chapter ends with Ruth returning to Naomi, telling her that Boaz said yes.

Now the next thing that Ruth does is rest and trust in Boaz's ability to redeem her and her family. How much more should we rest in the God who has already redeemed us? We already know that the debt was paid in full because of the resurrection of Christ on the third day. Shall we not be comforted in knowing that we have been redeemed and cannot lose that redemption?

Look at our lives. Surely the pain and suffering we experience here is miniscule in comparison to the glorious restoration we shall experience when the trumpets sound and our triumphant King steps down off the throne of peace. Will He not wipe away every tear? Will every knee not bow?

Will every tongue not confess that He is Lord? Friend, when that day comes, what will matter but our God?

I am in no way trying to downplay your pain and suffering. That emotion is real, and it matters. Your grievances are heard, and your tears are not unwarranted! All I ask is that you remember what is to come. Therefore, you cannot lament forever over the brokenness of the world, for that is *Tiny God Syndrome*. To weep over the rebellion of humanity, fall tiresome to the anguish of life, or grow angry at the sin of man is the right response, but you must not stay in that state. Friend, wipe your tears from your face, because if you know how big your God is, then you know He will restore the world to its former glory—but *better*! Do not weep without later rejoicing in the name of the Lord our God.

Finally, I want to go back to the overbearing weight of anxiety that seems to unceasingly tether to us. I recall seeing a movie called *A Beautiful Mind* when I was younger—probably around age twelve. Although I could understand the plot, I did not fully grasp the message of the story. It is based on the life of a man named John Forbes Nash Jr. who was a mathematical genius and a Princeton graduate. Throughout the film, John begins to meet several people when at Princeton. The viewer eventually learns (*spoiler alert) that the people he was meeting turned out to be imaginary. John was making these people up in his head and was found to have a condition in which he had created long-involved relationships with people that didn't exist. This then began to make John question what was real and what was fake. You can imagine at this time that John was having some major anxiety. Yet through some counseling and much mental toil, John's mental state is somewhat repaired—but he is never completely fixed. At the end of the movie, John's friend asks him, "Are they gone?" John responds, "No . . . and I don't think they'll ever leave. But the more I choose to ignore them, the more they leave me alone."

Friend, we cannot fully rid ourselves of the anxieties of this world. However, the more we choose to focus on the Lord rather than fixate on our problems, the more our worries will slowly diminish. This is by no means a permanent fix, but I say to you on this side of eternity that there are no permanent solutions. The only solution is the Lord our Savior Jesus Christ—the Messiah and the Burden Lifter. Lay your anxieties at the cross, and cast your burdens, no matter the size, at the feet of the Lord. Remember, the pain of this world is temporary, but God's love is eternal.

When talking to the new young adults minister, Kyle Jacobson (as I introduced in the introduction of this book), I asked this question: "Does anxiety tend to get better or worse as you age?" His response was similar to what I have said, but he had something quite interesting to say about Christian maturity. He directed me to Luke 5 and John 21. In Luke 5, we find the story of Jesus' first encounter with Peter. In the story, Peter is fishing and not having much luck. However, his tide begins to turn when Jesus tells him to recast his net into deeper water. Suddenly, Peter feels the net begin to break from the multitude of fish he has just caught. When he arrives at shore, Peter falls to his knees and says, "Go away from me."

In contrast, in John 21, we find Peter fishing with the disciples. (Keep in mind that this occurs after the death of Christ). We see Jesus' resurrected body on the shore, calling out to the men. He tells them to throw their nets on the right side of the boat rather than the left. Not knowing that this is the voice of the Son of Man, they do so. After casting the net, it becomes so full that they are unable to pull in the absurd amount of fish. Then John, while looking ashore, exclaims, "It is the Lord!" When Peter hears this, he immediately jumps overboard and aggressively swims toward the shore to meet Jesus.

Presented to us in these two passages is the same man but at different levels of spiritual maturity. The first time,

Peter is ashamed of his sin and does not even want the Lord near him. However, the next time, that same man is so desperate to get to the Lord that he jumps overboard and swims nearly one hundred yards. What does this show us? This presents a beautiful picture of maturity. Peter is starting to understand that what he needs most is God and cannot rely on any other means of salvation. It seems that as young believers, many of us are not so quick to run to the Lord as we are to things of this world. However, as maturity settles in and we are failed by things of this world, the appeal of Christ becomes easier to run to. The spiritually mature will find it a lot easier to run to the Lord because they have seen God's faithfulness over and over in their life and rely solely on the hope that is the resurrection of Christ. Therefore, anxiety may not change as you get older in terms of frequency, but as you spiritually mature, you will find yourself running more and more toward the Lord, who is the safe haven for your burdens.

5

THE CREATOR

In 2011 the Hubble Space Telescope discovered the most distant galaxy ever seen, about 13.2 billion light years from earth. To give some perspective about how far that is, a light year is the distance that light travels in one year (approximately 5.87 trillion miles). Our sun, which is 93 million miles from Earth, is a mere eight minutes away at the speed of light."[5]

Now let's take it in the completely opposite direction. Look at human anatomy and physiology. Your entire body is composed of cells, and all of these cells are composed of several different proteins, fats, and nucleic acids. Inside the nucleus of the cell is something known as the nucleolus. Inside of the nucleolus is a genetic code called DNA, but inside your DNA is the genetic code composed of nucleotides—separated in specific orders to make you, you. However, even smaller enzymes work on your DNA in something called replication, which is the copying of your DNA to complete various tasks such as the creation of new cells. Even more fascinating is that if you were to take all the DNA in your cells, it would be roughly the length of two times the diameter of the solar system. Now I mentioned earlier that there is a genetic code written on these strands of DNA. Therefore, it would be like reading every single book ever written one thousand times.

Our God is big enough to hold the entire universe in His hands and wise enough to create the smallest molecules in the world. He has created the stars in the night sky and the cells that make up your body. Amazing! Let me make this clear before I even start: I will fail at describing the majesty of the Lord because He is truly indescribable. I just want to spark an interest into the attempt to fathom such a Creator.

Yes, God has granted dominion to man over the land and animals (Genesis 1:26), but man has created discord amongst the Creator of Earth, and with that comes discord amongst His creation. Yet amid the hostility we find the supremacy of God. The authoritative nature of the Most High has only grown more dominant with the dissension of mankind. In the book *The Attributes of God*, Arthur W. Pink states the following:

> God's supremacy over the works of his hands is vividly depicted in Scripture. Inanimate matter, irrational creatures, all perform their Maker's bidding. At his pleasure the Red Sea divided and its waters stood up as walls (Exod. 14); and the earth opened her mouth, and guilty rebels went down alive into the pit (Num. 16). When he so ordered, the sun stood still (Josh. 10); and on another occasion went backward ten degrees on the dial of Ahaz (Isa. 38.8). To exemplify his supremacy, he made ravens carry food to Elijah (1 Kings 17), iron to swim on top of the waters (2 Kings 6:5), lions to be tame when Danial was cast into their den, fire to burn not when the three Hebrews were flung into its flames. Thus

"Whatsoever the Lord pleased, that did he in heaven, and in earth, in the seas, and all deep places" (Ps. 135:6).[6]

As a whole, we have grown proud of the self-made men and women society tells us to be. Yet we refuse to acknowledge a God who reigns supreme over all nations. The egregious lie and the bitter irony that states we are the rulers of the world quickly fall apart at the seams once we realize the divine authority of God. It is not until this realization that we can then allow our God to reverse the brokenness within the world. Therefore, without a divine supremacy, the children of God cannot rest. Charles Spurgeon wrote this when talking about the supremacy of God:

> There is no attribute more comforting to His children than that of God's Sovereignty. Under the most adverse circumstances, in the most severe trials, they believe that Sovereignty has ordained their afflictions, that Sovereignty overrules them, and that Sovereignty will sanctify them all. There is nothing for which the children ought more earnestly to contend than the doctrine of their Master over all creation—the Kingship of God over all the works of His own hands—the Throne of God and His right to sit upon that Throne. On the other hand, there is no doctrine more hated by worldlings, no truth of which they have made such a football, as the great, stupendous, but yet most certain doctrine of the Sovereignty of the infinite Jehovah. Men will allow God to be everywhere except on His throne. They will allow Him to be in His workshop to fashion worlds and make stars. They will allow Him to be in His almonry to dispense His alms and bestow His bounties. They will allow Him to sustain the earth

57

and bear up the pillars thereof, or light the lamps of heaven, or rule the waves of the ever-moving ocean; but when God ascends His throne, His creatures then gnash their teeth, and [when] we proclaim an enthroned God, and His right to do as He wills with His own, to dispose of His creatures as He thinks well, without consulting them in the matter; then it is that we are hissed and execrated, and then it is that men turn a deaf ear to us, for God on His throne is not the God they love. But it is God upon the throne that we love to preach. It is God upon His throne whom we trust.[7]

Through scripture and the world around us, we see the sovereignty of God. Inside of His sovereignty, humanity will find His divine wisdom. The wisdom of God extends beyond all understanding, it far surpasses the detrimental desires of mankind, and it fulfills the healthy desires that can only be found in Himself. Would a wise God not work out all things for the good of His creation and in doing so for the ultimate glorification of Himself? For the Creator has the right to do whatever He pleases with the creation. Therefore, would a sovereign God who is wise not plan all things according to His purpose, His purpose being to ultimately bring glory to Himself?

With that said, however, God does not require our praise. For the God of the universe has glorification in Himself that is the Trinity. For the Father glorifies the Son, the Holy Spirit glorifies the Father and the Son, and the Son glorifies the Father and the Holy Spirit (John 13:31-32). God merely invites us to bask in the glory that is His presence, which is the greatest gift we can receive as His creation.

God's wisdom and power work hand in hand to display His majesty and control over His creation. "His wisdom is profound, His power is vast" (Job 9:4). "Do you not know? Have you not heard? The Everlasting God, the LORD, the Creator of the ends of the earth does not become weary or tired. His understanding is inscrutable" (Isaiah 40:28). "Indeed, God is mighty; and he does not despise people, he is mighty, and firm in his intent" (Job 36:5). "Let the name of God be blessed forever and ever, for wisdom and power belong to Him" (Daniel 2:20). Is it not a comfort to know that God is both all-powerful and all-wise? For if any one of the two were unequal, then the resulting God would be frightening. Who could trust a God who was not all-wise but rash and often erroneous? For would that god not be one of dictatorship? Or if not tyranny, then would he not show a mere lack of concern for his creation? Likewise, who could find rest in a god that was all-wise but not all-powerful? For no hope could be found in such a creator, as the uncertainties of his divinity would constantly be in question.

J. I. Packer said the following about the wisdom and power of God: "Wisdom without power would be pathetic, a broken reed; power without wisdom would be merely frightening; but in God boundless wisdom and endless power are united, and this makes him utterly worthy of our fullest trust."[8] Peace is not found in a small God but in one who is omnipotent and omniscient. The God who is all-knowing and all-powerful is the God you can rest in. For there is no greater creator than one who has worked all things according to His purpose and has the infinite wisdom to do so in a perfect manner. Our God must be a big God in order for humanity to have hope and refuge in our future. A small God would only create insecurity amongst man that would divulge into detrimental anxiety, coating the already broken nature of mankind in a bitter poison known as despondency.

Wisdom does not mean a lack of human suffering. If the goal of the Lord is to bring ultimate glorification to Himself and to achieve such a task by showing us the love

He has for His creation, then great suffering must occur. For no man who ever suffered little loved much. Rather, the ones that know the pain of searing loss will in turn know the blessing of abundant love. Therefore one of the most paradoxical yet comprehensible things on earth is the idea of human suffering. Suffering is a harrowing yet beautiful sight. Suffering is a polluted yet cleansing endurance. Suffering is a strenuous yet necessary cause for the Christian's effect—that effect being the adoration of a God so willing to love His creation that He stepped down into the darkness that surrounded man and pulled Him out through the greatest act of love, sacrificial death.

My preacher told this story one time, and the previous sentence reminded me of it: There were two boys in Mississippi who were ages thirteen and ten. They were playing in the woods together, as they usually did before dinner time. But one day, after the sun had fallen, they did not make it home for dinner. Alarmed, the parents ran out into the woods to find their youngest stuck, waist deep in quicksand. Frantically panicking, the mother asked her son, "Where is your brother?" To which the son replied, "I am standing on his shoulders." Slowly humanity has fallen into death that swallows us up with a relentless grasp. Yet, in the midst of the tragedy, we see the beauty in the Savior Jesus Christ, who has come to take the place of the condemned.

Suffering is like a medicine: take too much, and it will kill you, but take too little, and there will be no effect. The appropriate amount must be taken. Aren't we glad to know that our God, the Creator of the Universe, who knows you personally and perfectly, is the Director of your suffering? He is like a skilled heart surgeon, knowing exactly how far to plunge the scalpel. Then, He removes the dirty broken heart of man and replaces it with a clean heart that renews the spirit (Psalm 51:10). "Oh, the depth of the riches of the wisdom and knowledge of God! How unsearchable his judgments, and his paths beyond tracing out!" (Romans 11:33). Just as children receive parental discipline or the painstaking word "no" that stirs anger and remorse in the adolescent heart, our heavenly Father disciplines us and tells us "no" so that we may grow and have a better "yes" to come.

If we look to John 15:1-17, it is there we find Jesus' allegory of the vine and the branches. Jesus reminds us that the Father "takes away every branch that does not bear fruit" (which are those who do not believe), and "every branch that does bear fruit he prunes, that it may bear more fruit." The word *prune* in the Greek translation can also mean "to clean." Therefore, the story points to a picture of suffering in the hands of a divine God in order to clean the dirty lives of man. He takes away things that may be harmful to us and exposes us to that which may hurt—but only to later reveal how great His love is for us and to work all things for our good. Not only does it show that suffering is helpful, but it shows how necessary it is. A vine cannot bear more fruit unless it is regularly pruned, and pruned well. Thus the suffering in a Christian's life is necessary in the sanctification process.

At this point, I want to propose a rhetorical question: Did God create man with the sole intention of us falling in order to show His love for us, ultimately giving Him more glory than He would have had, had He not let us fall? I ask this question not to stir strife amongst believers or grow anxiety in the hearts of anyone. Rather, I pose this question to spur thought into who God is. If He is truly in control of everything (which He is), then nothing could happen that was outside of God's control. Likewise, humanity would have never known the depth of love the Creator has for His creation had they not experienced sacrificial love. That sacrificial love could not have happened without a need for sacrifice. Therefore, redemption must take place; but keep in mind that redemption can vary depending upon the circumstance.

The redemption that took place was of the highest cost. Grace is free, not cheap. In a previous chapter we talked about the egregiousness of sin. Recall that stealing candy is deserving of eternal separation from God because of who He is. Now, think about all the sin of humanity dating from the beginning of the Fall to now. The ransom owed to save our damned souls was far greater than any amount man could ever fathom. It took God, Himself, dying, to settle our debt. The God of the universe died, and we killed Him. You will never find a sentence like that anywhere else except in Christianity. In that statement you find a love so radically magnificent which gives hope to the hopeless, life to the lifeless, and song to the speechless. It is the triumphant melody that reigns on high but would have never been so sweet without the pain of searing loss.

The gospel, for me, is not always this refreshing thing that makes me want to go out and conquer every day. Even in church, more times than not, I find myself losing focus or planning afternoon engagements. This, of course, is not due to any fault of the gospel; rather, it is my own sinful nature that does such a thing. There are times when the gospel sounds brand new . . . times when it refreshes me and reminds me of how brilliant our Lord is. One of those times was when I read the *Count of Monte Cristo*. It was then that I read a quote that well summarizes the idea of human suffering and divine love. It says,

> There is neither happiness nor misery in the world; there is only the comparison of one state with another, nothing more. He who has felt the deepest grief is best able to experience supreme happiness. We must have felt what it is to die . . . that we may appreciate the enjoyments of life. Live, then, and be happy, beloved children of my heart, and never forget, that until the day God will deign to reveal the future to man, all

human wisdom is contained in these two words,
Wait and Hope.[9]

Our hope is anchored in a God who died. Our
assurance is found in His resurrection. Our peace is in His
sovereign nature to accomplish these things.

6

THE AUTHORITY

A name is only as powerful as the man who owns it. For centuries, men have been called to make a name for themselves—to leave a legacy, if you will. Some men have done that in positive ways and others have accomplished this in tragic ways. Even POTUS (the president of the United States) holds weight in the title of president. Despite your political views, the president has authority because of their position and their name. It doesn't matter what you might think of him, he affects your life, whether you like it or not. That being so, how much more can be said about the name of Jesus. It does matter what you say about Jesus and who you say He is.

I heard a preacher once say that there is great power in the name of Jesus. *What exactly did he mean?* I wondered. Could it be that the actual name itself holds divine power? Could this be the reason that kings call upon the name of the Lord before battle? Is this why, in the midst of suffering and trial, we cry out the name of God? Or is it that the name was great because of the actions of Jesus? Is this why the rabbis of the Old Testament were so cautious to use the name of the Lord, because it held such power? Is this why most will still abbreviate the name of God YHWH—to display reverence and respect for the Lord?

Thousands of times per day, people call upon the name of Jesus in prayer. John 14:14 says, "If you ask me anything in my name, I will do it." What does this mean for us? Is it that God is willing to act as our personal genie? Does this then really put us in power over God because we call the shots? No, of course not. God is not our bank; He is our Father. How impersonal and shallow it is to view the God of the universe as your wish granter. When Jesus says in His name, He is not simply speaking of the physical aspect of His name alone, but He is speaking a testament to His character. If what you seek is not in alignment with the character and motives of God, then you will not receive what you ask for. We already know that God's motive is to bring glory to Himself, and He mercifully invites us to bask in that glory. Therefore, we are to ask not what only favors ourselves but what is in alignment with the will and character of God.

All of this, of course, highlights one key element, which is the authority of Jesus. God's authority is on display here as He is the one in control. Our God calls the shots from His throne and has the authority to give the people of God what they need.

If we take a look at Genesis 1:1, we find the verse most everyone knows: "In the beginning God created the Heavens and the Earth." What people might not notice is the word used for God here. Throughout the Bible, God shows us His many names; however, the name that is first presented in Genesis 1:1 is "Elohim." ("In the beginning *Elohim* created the Heavens and the Earth.") Why this name and not another? Well, *Elohim* translates to "mighty one" or "supreme." When the name is used, it is used in order to display authority and power. The creation of the heavens and the earth refers to all of creation. Thus He who is Elohim (supreme) rules over that creation. This points to the authority of God and provides an initial knowledge of His rule.

Although at this point, we have no other knowledge of who God is, we do know that He holds authority over everything. Therefore, when we later find out that our God is a benevolent God who loves us and wants a personal relationship with us, we rejoice. We have the ability to rejoice and we have comfort in knowing that it will last because nothing can overtake God—He is Elohim.

Oftentimes we remember the goodness of God but forget His authority. What good is a god who loves you if he does not have the authority to claim you? How then can a good father take care of his children if he is constrained by something or someone greater than him? There would be no rejoicing in a God who had no authority because the love provided would be weak. If a man who lives modestly and makes forty thousand dollars a year promises to give you five million dollars, you would be skeptical of his ability to do so. However, if Bill Gates or Warren Buffet were to promise you five million dollars, you would have more faith in them. Therefore, a small god with little authority has little security to offer. That is why in Genesis 1:1, *Elohim* is the first word used to describe God.

We must also look at the plurality of the word *Elohim*. The word in Genesis 1:1 encapsulates multiple people, but the verb *created* translates to "one being." The Trinity has always been present since the beginning of time. Thus the very same God that is Elohim is Jesus Christ. Jesus is God incarnate (God in the flesh). Jesus has all the authority of the Father, God of the universe.

Daniel, in chapter 7, has apocalyptic visions, which serve at the time to reassure God's people that God is still in control. In verses 13-14, Jesus is mentioned:

> *In my vision at night I looked, and there before me*
> *was one like a son of man, coming with the clouds*
> *of heaven. He approached the Ancient of Days and*
> *was led into his presence. He was given authority,*
> *glory and sovereign power; all nations and peoples*
> *of every language worshiped him. His dominion is*
> *an everlasting dominion that will not pass away,*
> *and his kingdom is one that will never be destroyed.*

In these verses we find hope in the midst of despair. It provided rest and assurance in the times of Daniel, and it provides rest and assurance in today's world as well. Today, Jesus, the Son of Man, is our hope. It is to Him that all glory, majesty, power, and authority have been given (Jude 25).

If we flash forward about six hundred years to Matthew 9, we find Jesus healing a paralytic. While Jesus was teaching, men removed the roof of the building Jesus was in and lowered a paralytic down before the Lord. It was after Jesus' recognition of the men's faith that He spoke: "Take heart, my son, your sins are forgiven" (Matthew 9:2). At this moment some were skeptical, calling it blasphemy. "For no one can forgive sins but YHWH" (v. 3), they said. But Jesus responds to them and says, "Why do you think evil in your hearts? For which is easier, to say, Your sins are forgiven, or to say, Rise and Walk? But that you may know that the Son of Man has authority on earth to forgive sins" (vv. 4-6). After He said this, Jesus told the man to "Rise," pick up his bed, and go home. Without hesitation, the paralytic rose and went home. This shows that Jesus has been granted authority in heaven and on Earth. Meaning that Jesus is the Son of Man. He is the very same Son of Man that is spoken of previously in Daniel 7 and the one who will be spoken of in Jude 25. God incarnate is Jesus Christ.

In healing a paralytic, Jesus is demonstrating His great authority that has been granted to Him from God the Father.

Also demonstrated is the forgiveness of sin. It is important to note that before even healing the man, Jesus forgives his sin. It was most likely unexpected for Him to do this because I'm sure the reason the men had brought their friend to Jesus was for him to be healed, but they were only looking for an outward expression of health. However, Jesus knows that the root cause of death, destruction, and disease is sin (Romans 5:12). Therefore, He did not do what the man might have wanted in the moment; He did what the man needed. Ultimately, He displayed His power, wisdom, and authority. Jesus need not ask permission to forgive sins because He has the authority of God the Father to do so: "And he has given him authority to execute judgment, because he is the Son of Man" (John 5:27).

"For even the Son of Man came not to be served, but to serve and to give his life as a ransom for many" (Matthew 20:28). Imagine you are with God in heaven. You are an angel, and you hear Him say, "I will go save the people of Earth. I will put on flesh and die for their ransom." If you heard this, you would surely question it. You might say, "For those are a wretched people, tied to their own desires and lusts. That place is nothing but a mere speck of dust in the universe You have so magnificently created. Why must You save people who seem so insignificant?" It is a valid statement. By no means does humanity deserve salvation, for we are a broken people and minute in comparison with the universe. God says we have value, and for that reason we become significant.

What is even crazier is that the God of the universe is serving those who ought to be serving Him. Is it not crazy that God kneeled at the feet of Peter and washed him clean? If you look at John 13, the God of the universe took the role of slave and scrubbed the dirty, broken feet of the disciples and said to them, "I must do this." For if God had not cleansed humanity, they would have surely died because the punishment against that which is holy is death, and the ransom is death upon Him who is the holiest of holy. Even so, could God not just snap His fingers to fix the problem?

If the God of the universe had not washed the feet of man, then we would have never known the depths to which His love grows. He is perfect, and His plans are perfect.

7
THE ADOPTION

I want them," she demanded. She pleaded with the agencies she had already fought so hard with. She knew who she was coming to get and did not fly halfway across the world to not get what was hers.

This is the story of a mother, a father, and their two adopted daughters. It had always been a desperate dream for Ann to have a baby of her own. She wanted to be a mom, and no one was going to stop her. Shortly after marrying Charlie, they decided they wanted to have children. Through various trials with doctors and failed attempts to conceive a child, Ann began to lose hope. She had always imagined holding her little girl or boy in her arms but now was starting to realize she might never have the opportunity. Charlie was also discouraged at the fact that he might never get to play catch with the son he always wanted or take his daughter to the daddy-daughter dance. All are simple things but sweet things that both of them desperately wanted.

They approached their pastor along with others at their church. It wasn't like they had not been praying. Many times over, they had prayed for a child but had not received one. It was in these moments the pastor of the church told Ann and Charlie that God may have other plans. "I know that's not always easy to hear," he said, "but there are other options." The pastor presented the possibility of adoption. He didn't tell them to make any rash decisions up front; however, he did tell them to pray about it.

After some time had passed and both of them had prayed about it, they decided they would look into adoption. No surprise, it was not an easy process. Miles of paperwork would have to be filled out, referrals had to be collected, and in the last stage they must travel to the foster home or orphanage themselves. After several months of hard work and patience, they got matched up with two twin girls from China. They were beautiful to Ann and Charlie, and they would not trade those girls for the world. With angst in their stomachs and nervous anticipation, they awaited the most crucial phone call of their life. The one that said either they could come pick them up or have to reapply and start the process all over. To their luck, the call was good news: they could come pick up their girls! Without hesitation, Ann and Charlie packed bags and booked the first flight they could to China.

Upon arrival, they immediately sought the agency and found it conveniently located near the airport. The only inconvenience was a ferry one must take to cross to the other side of the city in order to reach the agency. After shuffling their way through enormous amounts of people, they were able to get safely on and off the ferry. Finally at the agency, they were ready to meet the girls.

Without hesitation, they asked the woman working to bring the girls to them. The woman solemnly said that the girls they had been paired with are no longer available for adoption. Ann quickly grew angry and wanted to know why the girls they have planned to adopt this whole time had now been taken. After back and forth arguments and ill attempts to communicate, the woman told them that the girls are to be sold. They were to be sold as a pair to another agency. The agency offered Ann and Charlie several other children, but they both knew exactly who they came for and were not leaving without their girls.

Angered and outraged, the parents demanded to see their children and threatened to sue and expose the corrupt agency's dealings. After several more hours of back and forth, they released the girls. Finally the moment had come when they would first be united with their children. They were adorable, both of them holding hands, walking out with bows in their hair. To Ann and Charlie, they were the most precious things in the world, and no one could keep them apart. They presented the girls with gifts and matching Hello Kitty backpacks. The girls grinned ear to ear and couldn't stop smiling. They finally had a home, but more than that, they had someone who would fight for them, love them, and be there for them no matter what.

This is a beautiful story, and anyone who hears it fights alongside the parents and the children. This makes us angry at the agency who wanted to steal them away. This makes us rejoice when we hear that the parents have been united with their children. *Why?* This is not just the story of Ann and Charlie or the two girls—this is the story of Christians everywhere. We have all been lost, alone, and broken, with nowhere to run, nowhere to hide, nowhere to rest. However, we were never forgotten. Held captive by the enemy, we cried and begged for someone to come rescue us. We knew that this was not our home, and we longed for our true home. We needed a Father to come claim us as His own. However, we could not leave, for the evil one had a grip on us.

Yet our God did what we never expected and contradicts every other religion. Instead of us trying to free ourselves from the wretched grasp of sin and work our way to God, God worked His way to us. And He didn't just travel from small town Tennessee to China. No, He left His kingdom in heaven and traveled to Earth, and He came for a purpose. For our God came to take back what was His. He came to redeem the children of God—except this time, the withholder would not let go so easily. The evil one said if you want your creation you'll have to pay for them. God knew this would happen and accepted what He must do. Taking our place, He gave His life for ours. The most paradoxical act in history was the greatest act of love. We are the most broken things on Earth: dirty, wretched, and vile. To anyone but God we would be unredeemable. Keep in mind that we did not love our God till He first loved us. Therefore, God showed His love for us at the cross.

In God's infinite wisdom, He planned to redeem us so that we may know how much He loves us. Ephesians 1:5 says, "He predestined us for adoption to Himself as sons through Jesus Christ, according to the purpose of His will." Our adoption was no accident. God's plan to redeem us has always been there, since "before the foundations of the earth" (Ephesians 1:4). For this is the predestined will of God. It's amazing that the God of the universe has loved us "before the foundations of the world." For only a big God could work such things according to His purpose. Only a big God could have adopted us in such a magnificently beautiful plan. Our adoption is not weighed on what we have done or what we might do. Our adoption was destined by God in eternity; therefore, we cannot lose our salvation once we have it. For if an eternal God sees eternity and claims something to be His, then that thing will be His for eternity. Our adoption was decided not based on merit, status, or any self-worth, for our adoption was decided before the foundations of the earth. No one shall snatch you from the grasp of the almighty Father, because this is the almighty plan of God.

We must remember that we were adopted for a purpose. We were adopted to honor and glorify God. This adoption is for God's glorification. Remember that our purpose in creation is to honor and glorify God, so the best blessing one can receive is to be able to honor and glorify Him. It is a loving thing that God allows us to worship Him and praise Him, because that is what brings us ultimate joy.

If you say that God sounds self-centered in this, then good, He should be at the center! But you cannot say He is unloving. Think about it this way: whether a person admits it or not, we all long for the repair of the broken relationship found in Genesis 3. If you don't believe me, do this: Take any meaningful relationship you might have or have had. You want that relationship to grow, and you desire a profound understanding of your love for that person. You want to know how they are feeling. You want to give them everything you believe they deserve. You want to exalt them and lift them up. Now take that relationship and imagine shattering it. You just really screwed up and hurt that person in ways that you can't fathom. From then on, the only thing you can think of is restoring that relationship. Longing for how it used to be.

C. S. Lewis said, "Do fish complain of the sea for being wet? Or if they did, would that fact itself not strongly suggest that they had not always been, or would not always be, purely aquatic creatures?"[10] Why do we as humans complain of brokenness and urge for restoration of relationships? The most logical answer is because we long for the restoration of the ultimate relationship with our God. For God to restore that relationship, thus allowing us to fulfill our purpose of glorification of the Father, is the most loving thing He can do. To be able to commune with Him is the most joy one can experience because nothing is better than Him.

8

THE CURE

Preparing for college can be a stressful time for anyone. There are numerous amounts of things to be considered. Maybe it's determining monetary factors that cause you to choose one school over another. Perhaps the location and the commute makes it closer to home. Or the one you'd hear more often than expected was that the Greek life is just so much better. All of those things should be considered and weighed appropriately.

I believe teachers, parents, and other mentors do a good job of expressing how to decipher between what best suits you. For example, there are hundreds of free online websites alone that can match you with your dream school in seconds. Everyone tells you what you need for your dorm room. They will banter on and on about how to stand out and how to get plugged into various groups. There's all sorts of information provided to you via parents and instructors about how to find the college for you.

Unfortunately, one of the things I rarely hear elaborated on or even mentioned is how to find a church home in college.

The most I ever hear mentioned is, "You should try and find a church when you go to college." Beyond that, there are no workshops on church homes and how to find one. Even if there are, they aren't directed at the appropriate audience. The seventeen-, eighteen-, and nineteen-year-olds are the ones who most dominantly need to hear about what to look for in a church. We need to hear about red flags that might steer us away from a church. We need to hear the questions we should ask if we're at a new church. We need to be taught about finding community in a church and the danger of being in a church that does not have strong fellowship.

Although I have not heard much teaching on how to find a church, there was a sliver of advice offered to me that has stuck with me. A man once told me that when I'm looking for a church, I need to ask the leadership one question: "What is God?" If the response does not pertain or mention the holiness of God, then you don't need to be at that church. Above all things, God is holy, and without His holiness, all else is lost. The church that does not teach on God's holiness is a church that is lost.

If we do not mention the wrath of God, how then are we to know the depths of His love? I grow tired of the thought that there are churches out there that proclaim God as loving above all other attributes. Even more so, I am displeased to hear about churches that never cover the loving attributes of God.

There are three types of churches that I have seen, and only one of them is teaching in the correct method:

1. The first church highlights all things good. They fixate on the love of God. This fills you with warm feelings and good emotions. However, these emotions are only temporary and leave you longing for something deeper. When the bad times happen, and they will, you start to question how powerful

God really is and His love for you. Suddenly He doesn't seem so close anymore.

2. The second church highlights the wrath of God. They try to strike fear into the congregation in order to make sure they straighten up and follow God's commands. Unfortunately, this only causes distress and worry amongst believers. It causes them to develop a distrust with God—the very same distrust that the first church experienced, just through different circumstances.

3. The third church does something different. First, they present the holiness of God and the foolish behavior of mankind. They show how you deserve hell and separation from God, with no chance of self-cleansing. However, they tell of the perfect plan of God to redeem what was lost and fix what was broken. They speak of an intercessor provided by God. They assure you of God's love in the fact that He is merciful. Then, they display a perfect God, executing perfect judgment, wrath, and love, all at the same time. This brings lasting comfort to you because this shows God's control over this world without diminishing His love for you. This God is bigger than the first two church's god because this God is able to show His power and wisdom alongside His love and forgiveness.

I have seen all three churches, and the people who seem to have the most comfort and least anxiety are the people who are fed a teaching full of God's attributes, with none of them overshadowed. They have a good understanding of God's wrath and its importance. For if there is no wrath of God, then there is no detestation of sin—creating an imperfect god. God's perfection demands His wrath. We must remember the sin nature that is within us. Our iniquity has made us enemies of the Father. If you worship the one true God, His wrath should cause us to tremble, and the mere thought of it will shake the foundations of Earth.

Furthermore, the fullness of His love would not be there if it had not first been highlighted by wrath. How great is it that the God of the universe looks upon sin with contempt, for it is the sin that binds us to our sorrow. The most loving thing God can do is set us free from that which consumes us. To merely forgive and forget is not God's way, for this would make His love conditional and His promises frail. Therefore, God supplied an intercessor that would satisfy His wrath, while freeing the captives of Satan. It is because of this that the third church is able to understand how magnificent God is in His holiness, while they rejoice in the richness of His love. A God of this stature provides security.

To go throughout your spiritual journey and never dwell on the wrath of God would be a disservice. Even more so, to strip a congregation of teachings on the wrath of God would be an abomination. For it is written that "You should fear: Fear him who, after your body has been killed, has authority to throw you into hell. Yes, I tell you, fear him" (Luke 12:5). God's judgement and wrath are aimed upon those who oppose Him. Those who oppose Him are the ones who have sinned. Consequently, there is an urgency to speak truth and preach the news of this God—that being news of His wrath and justice, then His love and forgiveness. Do not lower the power of your God by only speaking of His love. For first and foremost we serve a holy God.

Finally, I want to circle back to the horrid disease that is *Tiny God Syndrome*. TGS suffocates us and makes us weaker by the second. It is the reason we distrust. It is the reason we complain. It is the reason we worry. However, at the center of all our discrepancies can be found the root of our issue. Initially, our downfall is sin, but what holds us there is our small view of God. The inability to see how big God is, is a detriment upon our soul.

But the cure is simple. The cure is to live our lives in accordance with John 3:30: "He must increase, but I must decrease." We must relinquish our pride and unbind our shackles, for there is no hope except in Jesus Christ. Every day, we must continue to seek to know who God is. We should never shy away from what may scare us or confuse us but always seek truth that is found in Him. For the Spirit of God will work through us if we allow Him. Allow God to renew our hearts of stone into hearts of flesh (Ezekiel 36:26).

We will continue to fall into the trap of *Tiny God Syndrome*; however, He is faithful to finish the work He has started in us (Philippians 1:6). For there is no greater security than God, and there is no other way to view Him besides big. Our suffering is real, and as a repercussion, the pain is real. And the only solution to our suffering is Christ and placing Him above all. Therefore, whenever I think about the gospel and center my life around that, my relationships deepen and grow stronger with a new perception on love that culture cannot reproduce or comprehend. This acknowledgement of God at the center of my life and not something else relieves all the pressure of my emotional, physical, and spiritual relationships with others. Therefore I feel closest to others when I am closest to God, and I am closest to God when I am receptive to the gospel. I am receptive to the gospel when I am most humbled in a reliant love, and I am in the most reliant of loves when I have a small view of myself. I have a small view of myself when I have a truly magnificent, omniscient, omnipotent, omnipresent, big view of God. Our first steps to security and comfort is realizing that there is no security or comfort apart from the God who provides it.

I mentioned previously the devotion I gave on Isaiah 6. I spoke of the robe that encompassed the whole temple and how this speaks to God's holiness, which shows our separation from God. It shows us that if we were to present even the most devout servant of God, they would fall short of righteousness and could do nothing but curse themselves, realizing their much-deserved death (Isaiah 6:4-5). Yet amongst the shame and guilt, there comes hope from God.

The seraphim flies down and places a hot coal on the unclean lips of Isaiah, telling him that his sins are atoned for (Isaiah 6:6-7). The story presents a very clear picture in a very particular order. First the holiness of God is shown through a vision given to Isaiah. Second, there is a realization of the mightiness of God and how big He truly is. Third, there is a correct alignment of perspective when Isaiah recognizes his worth in comparison to God's. Fourth, there is a forgiveness that can only be offered from a holy God Himself. Fifth, there is rejoicing in the name of the Lord for all He has done, and there is a strong urge to do His will. Sixth, you leave with comfort and security and blessings, knowing that the God of the universe has redeemed you and calls you His child.

There is no better order to know God. If you have a small view of God, then you'll always have a small view of your worth. To truly know how big God is, is to know how much He loves you. The bigger the God, the deeper the love.

I try as much as possible to check up on my friends and ask how they are doing; however, I fail at this frequently. But when I do get to talk with them, it's always special. When I asked a friend of mine how they were doing spiritually one time, they replied, "Not well." They then went on to explain how they felt about God and how He just seemed way too good to be true. They could not believe that the God of the universe looked at them and counted them worthy. After about five minutes of explaining what they had done and how guilty they felt, they finally said, "I can't believe that God can forgive someone like me."

For some odd reason, I had a quote pop in my head that I heard a while back. Excitedly realizing how applicable it was, I smiled back at my friend and said, "Are you bruised, be of good comfort; He calls you. Conceal not your wounds, open all before Him and go to Christ, for there is more mercy in Him than sin in you." I, of course, butchered the quote that I later realized was from a man named Richard Sibbes, but they got the point.[11]

Friend: Yes, we have a big God who is holy and worthy of all praise, honor, and glory. However, do not discredit your worth. For He has called you by name and redeemed you. He is with you till the end of your days and forever more.

Isaiah 43

But now, this is what the Lord says—
he who created you, Jacob,
he who formed you, Israel:
Do not fear, for I have redeemed you;
I have summoned you by name; you are mine.
when you pass through the waters,
I will be with you;
and when you pass through the rivers,
they will not sweep over you.
When you walk through the fire,
you will not be burned;
the flames will not set you ablaze.
For I am the Lord your God,
the Holy One of Israel, your Savior;
I give Egypt for your ransom,
Cush and Seba in your stead.
Since you are precious and honored in my sight,
and because I love you,
I will give people in exchange for you,
nations in exchange for your life.
Do not be afraid, for I am with you;
I will bring your children from the east
and gather you from the west.
I will say to the north, 'Give them up!'
and to the south, 'Do not hold them back.'
Bring my sons from afar

and my daughters from the ends of the earth—
everyone who is called by my name,
whom I created for my glory,
whom I formed and made."

ENDNOTES

1   APA.org/news/press/releases/2000/12/anxiety

2   Businessinsider.com/cdc-teenage-gen-z-american-suicide-epidemic

3   James Flynn. *Are We Getting Smarter? Rising IQ in the Twenty-First Century.* Cambridge, IL: Cambridge University Press, 2012.

4   Careynieuwhof.com/episode187/

5   Andy Ramos, Exploregod.com/articles/how-big-is-god

6   Arthur Walkington Pink. *The Attributes of God.* New ed., Grand Rapids, MI: Baker Books, 2006.

7   Charles Spurgeon. Spurgeon.org/resource-library/sermons/divine-sovereignty/#flipbook/

8   J. I. Packer. *Knowing God.* 20th ed., Downers Grove, IL: InterVarsity Press, 1993.

9   Alexandre Dumas. *Count of Monte Christo.* NY: Grosset & Dunlap, 1922.

10   C. W. Lewis. Goodreads.com/quotes/1364053-c-s-lewis-in-his-second-letter-to-me-at-oxford

11   Richard Sibbes. *The Bruised Reed.* Philadelphia, PA: Presbyterian Board of Publication, 2007.

For more information, or to connect with author Jake Walker, email: *TinyGodSyndrome@gmail.com*

CPSIA information can be obtained
at www.ICGtesting.com
Printed in the USA
JSHW030856300321
13042JS00001B/1

9 781613 147467